C000066879

# Seder

Adam Kammerling

**Out-Spoken Press**
London

Published by Out-Spoken Press,
Unit 39, Containerville
1 Emma Street
London, E2 9AH

First edition published 2020
ISBN: 978-1-8380211-4-6

Typeset in Adobe Caslon
Design by Patricia Ferguson
Printed and bound by Print Resources

Out-Spoken Press is supported using public funding by the National
Lottery through Arts Council England.

Supported using public funding by
**ARTS COUNCIL
ENGLAND**

# Seder

For Walter and Herta Kammerling

# Contents

| | |
|---|---|
| in the grass | 1 |
| so tell us | 2 |
| what faith | 3 |
| let us say | 4 |
| we return to when | 5 |
| for my grandfather the demob centre | 6 |
| look | 7 |
| emerging in Theresienstadt | 8 |
| practice | 9 |
| blood. darkness. | 10 |
| *it is not propaganda's task* | 11 |
| but for the louse | 12 |
| thousands | 13 |
| I once read | 14 |
| we return to when | 15 |
| orange orange orange orange | 16 |
| now I am | 18 |
| in the moment | 19 |
| when I have drunk less | 20 |
| except my brothers used to watch me | 21 |
| it is nothing | 22 |
| Schwerbelastungskörper | 23 |
| before the kilning of the planets | 25 |
| through water | 26 |

swimming 27

where is safe when 28

orange 29

swimming 30

to get away 31

*why is this night different* 32

now I'm throwing 33

the baker 34

my horsefly 35

then a man then a man 36

sssh 37

did you know 38

I select my own 39

simply 40

substances deadly to goldfish 41

I am watching 42

onto this scene 43

notice 44

my mum wanted girls 45

the river is where 46

now I know 47


Notes 49

Acknowledgments 51

Titles are included as reference points, and as bridges. While each poem can be taken individually, they belong to this lineage of texts.

pl. *Seders*, or *Sederim*. Judaism. A ritual feast commemorating the exodus of the Jews from Egypt held on the first nights of Passover. Origin of Seder Hebrew: seder – order, arrangement.

they declared our blood

the wrong shade

I was not murdered here with Aunt Ruth

I pick up a beetle with two fingers

                    watch its belly palpitate

there is a goldfish in the horse pond

a white stork stood at the barracks

**so tell us**

Reverend Father in this school assembly of
dust and new smells how you found god in the Cold
War's failing liver; the jungle training your eye to pick
skulls through the scope from fifty metres drop bodies
through windows tell us how you came back changed
married your sweetheart for a dowry of cornbread and
then your daughter snatched from school by a man
you knew he took her for two days nearly
ending your life in half-knowing your knuckle-pit
screaming *rifle in the closet ammo in the drawers*

*rifle     rifle     rifle     rifle*     tell us
father that you crouched darkly in his garden your
face shoeblack blurred to pop his head like a grape
this whole gymnasium's fraying their sleeves tell us
your index finger opened and then closed the glass
circle to make the wall wet with him but you won't
tell us how she came back changed and you father
stroke the hair lock from her face but the screaming
*bushes to bathroom window* but the equation that
could tie his brain into a permanent zero but faith

## we return to when

we set this cup of salted water

this parsley-sprig lambshank this tower

of cinnamon and apple sultana

when this circle of bodies is seated and unseated a circle

in this table's centre a glass bowl its algae'd

castle and pump that whirrs

its small carp flickering orange and two candlesticks like sentinels

now we are lighting the candles

returning to when we set coasters and cloth white stretched

underneath as we hand out

prayerbooks our bodies folding in half asking *why*

*is this night different to all other nights* all other nights replying

## for my grandfather the demob centre

where the war is finished for him
returning the heavy wool coat that scratched under packs
and belts of ammo receiving
payment and civvies off racks and official papers returning to his name
Kammerling on all official papers his Austrian Jewishness
panic-struck under ambiguous skin
now plainly in paybook and medical records plainly in all official papers
returning his signature *Kerrison*
returning to sign on the dotted line his name of his parents and sisters
unhidden the officer asks him *spell it*
each letter emerging Germanic vowelled the officer noting them down
the officer looking up from his page pen-hand a humming
bird at no flower

       *you know you don't need to change it*
his pen-hand a bough about to break my grandfather
returned on official papers his parents and sisters and
this neat man with wet looking hair a voice that moves carefully
is leaning across the table between them  *No cost*

      *no legal implication simply don't change it back*

**look**

Kammerling is not a common surname

on memorials

where names drape the walls

look for Kammerman

      Kammersch

      Kammerle

*the act of remembering is*

in stillness the shared root

*its own justification*

## emerging in Theresienstadt

the letters arched over his office

*Kammer* translation: *Chamber n. (German)*

in this camp where a bureaucrat signed warrants over lunch

how many chambers to commit our name to this

*Kammer* where his pens leaned in their tins and pictures of his kids

pumpernickel crumbs a saucy card deck

how many rooms to ruin a surname starting

with this *Chamber* an archway its private space

its concrete cube nearly pitch black but for the hole in the roof that

lets in

its cylindrical iron that holds tightly

sound waves reflecting off hard tiled surfaces to return to

your signature                    *Kerrison*

a terraced street: two rooms and

an outhouse in Kent or Reading          *Kerrison*


do not let your hand

denounce your origins on the dotted line

in the grocers the bank your hostel      *unchristian*


bricks persuade windows it's funny

how the hand follows itself

into signature


what spells your unEnglishness      *Kammerling*

the beating truth; your hand

its cornet of ink

**blood. darkness.**

frogs.   boils.   we return to

*this night different to*

ten prints on a napkin this table turning

on the red wine's surface   disease.   flies.

how the lamb's blood adheres to mint leaves

how dates and nuts form pyramids that we built

*other nights* a circle

tonight we eat pyramids with our hands

scoop with the thumb onto matzos these hands;

five-pillared temples shook mint and mint shook its leaves

over doorframes the angel relaxing its garrote vil at the smell

# it is not propaganda's task

*to be intelligent*
a nest of vipers in the garden *its task is to lead to success*
in Grandpa's dreams; his son's face
and the black ribbon retreating

he brought his spade down twelve times
an interventionist deity as those in mythologies
which is what this is becoming
the legend of Grandpa and the vipers

except this actually happened except it turns out
there was only one snake so the story has changed
he said I knew from its head that it was venomous
and by its head we can assume the balaclavas

of Combat 18 there were leaflets
circulated by the neighbourhood where Grandpa did fight
the balaclava'd nest of snakes bringing a stick down on their skulls
emptying their venom into black knit their last slurs

barely audible he says *it feels very cruel* and we joke
that he should have written to the adder asking it to vacate
on the phone Grandpa and I draft the letter
so there was a snake and Grandpa did kill it

# but for the louse

<pre>
in the museum    his master looming over
                 craven-faced Christless skull-skinny one
                 -eyed see in the sockets cavity? swarming        I learn propaganda
                 bodies the segmented bodies he homes
                 enflamed and blooming black bile teeth
                 shake vomiting old ways he rubs his hands
                 hacks while a church evaporates to steam
         by      wetting his crook-back the louse commands      artists
                 spread your phlegm over Christian property
who knew          which insects you had no choice but to
                 obey locusts bully in their numbers            how
                 mosquito mainlines your bedblood silence
                 but for its arsenic peck they'll be our death    a screenprint
works            from sky inky thoraxes in thousands
</pre>

12

# thousands

like how the painter

prompts children to remake the camp

in her lessons the use of colour

and scale shrinks an SS guard to a thumb

all the features gone from his face

the space between empties children's own rain

on the camp from their hands

lacing a rainbow or gripping the pencil like an axe

1

2

　　　　3

how their parents tell them be good for teacher

for this quiet play this sprouting in secret:

how thousands of paintings and drawings

in Terezín before

their bodies were removed how they left

parts of themselves to escape how they escaped

how none escaped

---

1 *I learnt to teach by listening / to paintings and painter's books / loving how / to*
   *make hair feel real to dapple light / paint water wet*

2 *like a scientist simulating / normalcy: we make*

3 *marks as humidity / and mineral uptake /*

# I once read

a doctor's hypothesis putting forward
a glass of water with an 'I love you' note
freezes more beautifully than one without
as if water is listening that it smiles
his theory has been disproven but I have my own
am investigating how loss can drown how
absence is also a flooding there is
yet another hypothesis: self injury

is congruent with negative feelings
in regards to self image not in regards to
this image wall-mounted and held to
not this photograph of line A and B and
a boy in dust-cap and shorts with his sisters
not this boy unambiguous in silver nitrate
knowing he must be brave please
for his sisters
not both his baby sisters

## we return to when

we set coasters and cloth this cup of salted water

as we hand out prayerbooks asking *is this night always*

returning to the man who falls asleep on the train

the man who doesn't look Jewish

the one about the man who is too honest at this table

there is always a portal to a joke's beginning

it reminds me of Grandpa always returning to

the dates of when the details are too much I will not repeat

they are repeated enough in one brass pulse stretched under

our every arrival to when there is set these candles

this horseradish cut finely this glass holding its small fire

**orange orange orange orange**

orange the beds of unslept eyes
orange the pebble's puncture through glass
orange the fire and ember (obviously) and lava
orange the line on a knuckle

tourists demean onto gravel all orange
the caffeinated gibber of bus-exhaust its awful taste
orange the phlegm that comes at the end of something easy
the beginning of something worse

orange the edge of floor-tom its rusted blood against drumskin
orange the electrode-flooded vacuum its glass cup
orange the drumskin

the orange heatwave broken by an unreal rain

orange this hangover wasping the skull for a life
orange the firm-joint calliper framing a young girls head
orange the unvenomous snake feeding
frozen mice in its gullet because
orange the bricks

orange the twenty-eight brick buildings the twenty-three kilos

the five hundred thousand orange

the goldfish in the pond at Auschwitz

orange the trough the tank the pond there is

a goldfish in the pond there is

a goldfish there is a goldfish there is

a goldfish there is a goldfish there is a goldfish

## now I am

lifting down into the runway's compass

only ever unclipping my seatbelt

I want to see my name held by a stranger

floating into inactivity I want an airport in the desert

yellow cars in a line it's amazing

how a snake's appetite is quantum

how leprosy lives in the pocket; a bouquet

of collapsible flowers

I want to tell you

that a human eye socket holds

a clumsily poured double

that Moses raised his hand

and the Hebrews were winning in battle so he lowered it and

then they were not

**in the moment**

high-pitched and circling the woman
beside me not hearing I can't let it go
the jewish conspiracy
media banks zionist world order
her hand on my knee like spilt fondue
can't let the weight and the heat of it go
you're the problem not skinhead not nazi but cool
Finsbury Park neighbour you're the problem
and someone sings a Christmas carol
to defuse but I can't stop *it's not funny*
can't stop *for fuck's sake* this becoming a scene
will not help Grandpa my voice
is a kettle cooked to the scale

I am replying calmly on the train

to line up

to unpick gently her views

so a siren is not stalking the aisle screaming

along the Valley Road for my Grandpa an ambulance

outside our house him stretchered a crooked bridge

between paramedics

his fall to concrete crackling

through rooms medics helping but I cannot

here on this train all drunk around me and listening in

I am not replying calmly

I am not stopping

to say I'm sorry really I'm sorry so everyone says

no! you have nothing to be sorry for

drawing panels from comics we knelt
three of us hushed watching my pencil
pressing the swell of biceps punching
or soldiering intense pain I imagined
that if I experienced superhuman hurt
I would grit my teeth and flex my fingers
that pain would arch me like a masseuse
evoking an unpronounceable sound:
GRRAAAAAKKKRRRRGGGHGGH
that I might have to be restrained so
I am surprised when thirty years later
I cannot erase a mistake and rather than
bulge like an onion I drop to my knees
and quietly do not process
not crying or shouting but watching
my useless hands which followed the
lines of superhumans copying what
burst from the panel as my brothers
watched: the picture coming on slow
emerging over the rubbed-out rails
the light dimming until I can't

**it is nothing**

to be sorry                    in Berlin

nothing to be sorry      in Prague

nothing to be sorry      in Krakow

in Oswiecim

Ravensbrück          Theresienstadt

Bergen-Belsen

there is a

## Schwerbelastungskörper;

cylindrical block of concrete
Schwerbelastungskörper; sinking inch
by grey inch unready today
I can only help my grandfather by talking
about Austrian food; knurdle kugel kipful listening
to jokes that all begin *it reminds me*
*of the one about the man* listening
how to drain keffir today's challah review
memories that flake edges of crust off the loaf
as you saw the lightest rain
hospital pond under trees goldfish
rise to the surface for crumbs
driving home in the golden hour
a phone call from Germany
the weight of a single pillar

there is a goldfish

**before the kilning of the planets**

into order

a satsuma drops                         from its bush

bowing low with fruit

it sinks            pith already petrifying

to a porcelain rose of fish bone

at the pond's floor                    it scales

air            and sky congeal

into fins                    a mouth

but the            quiet of underwater

a fossil to open the ear                    only

oxygen                    hydrogen

half truth

rushes

25

## through water

they know that
starlings learnt to murmur by following fish
eels squids the whale
that swallowed Jonah haunts the Bay of Biscay
learned its own testament before
any word could be scratched
hand to stick to mud
not *law* not *yoke* not *dominion*

they

take two                    pebbles

    into          their cheeks

gravity there

so            water will

bend a scroll            round

their cornea's    curves

collect          the river

an alphabet

where is safe when

still Blue Heron would kill them all

so Goldfish hides in the colder corners of their pond / on pebbles they taste the land / a print smudged / the way a heron's shadow falls rising / the feathered head of a lightning bolt / curious fish turned to salt licks for wanting to see / no defence against Heron's bullet neck / sulphur on Sodom's Quaker hamlet / burns their green towers their white bones boils the black jelly in their skulls / drunk and cruel / and careless / angels rain fire like dogs spray piss / a growl sounds not unlike the release of urine / a knife moving through water makes no sound

## orange

what comes into the blood what is shared
through the body its every island; elbows and
arches-of-feet orange its own song:
fire / lava / satsuma

the most fire I've seen it was by the sea
in Sydney it rained ash from the bushfires
tide frothing like a sick dog
the tributary breathing its flowering gum

**swimming**

they draw skeleton

leaves down        from

the surface

a        tail that moves

like      the air

above

forests

burning

## to get away

Goldfish folds in half
disappears text into spine
their body
is one long successful escape

they remember predators the taste
stalking through water; pike eel gull
brain primitive
they remember with fins
the Jin Dynasty in China
the forbidden colour yellow they can tell you
of wedding gifts and ornamental ponds
of circus wagons and coconuts stood for the shy
tombola the hot hands of children

remember with their convex lens
mares dipping circles
into green sky the changing taste
of algae a silence
that fell one winter

*why is this night different*

when there is set this shoe horn's grain suspended

in wood and this shelf at eye-level when there is set

rose-quartz a salt lick an ammonite we touch for its segmented feel

the woodchip-paper the shoehorn the space in yellowish columns

each its own tangible body the white cloth stretched under

our arrival to when there are candles set this glass bowl and our guest

in water orangely moving in circles weighing stones to remember

the mineral taste of arriving from water with Hebrew

now we are lighting the candles

our grandparents are holding us in both hands

## now I'm throwing

a fistful of dirt onto Erica's coffin I feel too young

to perform this act unsombre in my mismatched suit

the rabbi is watching and it is raining which is fitting or maybe

it isn't and my memory has added this detail like a movie

it is raining so whatever falls is washed

and soaked away and the rabbi is watching

me watching Grandpa weeping into his hands

I never thought what it was to lose a sister I want to see

a picture of Erica when she was younger

a strange feeling to reach for memory and hold nothing

like leaning into a fall blindfolded; the stomach jumps

# the baker

*in the museum*

*learn*

*our bodies*

*destroy*

kneads his dough with rank feet
it brings him no joy his bent-backed shape
steps in Jew-sweat printing the yeasty clump
he steps in his corn's hardskin his own bull-
neck buttocks teeth all smushed in his tread
each heel-punch he feels in his lungs the air
crackling closed he gains density body
doubling in size proving slow He is bread
he is all breads: rye soda chapati
knows a thousand years barely sustaining
escape: nighttime matzos stashed in packs
fleeing pharoahs and the mob's hottest fires
gaining! yeast mother gulps down oxygen
no Red Sea to fold itself in Europe

*the tools*

*to*

*were*

*pleasing*

*to the eye*

**my horsefly**

you were flying swooping kissing
awareness to my allergic face
your saliva commanding my histamines to it
bones felt now in their tubes I am back
inside my bones and can feel my teeth's enamel
inside my teeth my skin
hot and filling up my skin my eyes
my lungs' cauliflower pockets
gulps of hypervent I am back
inside the delousing house the mass grave
noting numb-mouthed
that numbness is rarely unfelt you taught me
it lights up a pocket of cold an epiphany
on all fours draining into the earth
this earth taking me back inside soaking me up
horsefly you were swooping your lines
gone so quick I am ashamed

then a man seeing red plaiting his fist            *I'm*
through my collar dragged up into
his flat into red and gold cushions                *struggling*
into a mirror he is showing me what                *to breathe*
trespassing means revealing                        *I'm*
upholstery photos brass clocks'                    *asthmatic*
chiming to show me betrayal
is the inside of a flat at midnight                *I need*
a nightgown and two dogs barking                   *ventolin*
the police on their way so how                     *please*
to escape a night-gown this private
upstairs I am lying myself
awkwardly down in his lounge a
dead child dividing the carpet                     *let*
awkwardly lying across both their
futures in his wife's bleary eyes

**sssh**


        we return to when

we        see nighttime

        closing a blunt force      trauma

        around the table      set

inside      the porthole it barks      from

        the street's dark body it barks

        how a brick enters      how

    a    wounded      stag

        rises from its woodpile

        great barrel of bone fitting neatly the mould

of        roof: a peelable      rind

        moment of absolute

    *sssh*


        how a brick

        threatens to un   fold

        the rafters exhale another      room's

        lamps

antlers     grasping

        in the windows the street


        it barks

*in the museum*                                                    *I learn*

'Mordechai breastfed Esther!

the men cross–dress! lactate! and can vanish!

by planting a menstrual blood–soaked apple.

God–smote the men bleed from their bellends!

and navels! and arses! divine vengeance

lightning'd their hinder parts for killing Christ'

the annual swarthy and goateed gathering

for Christian murder begins with these holes

*of the blood*

poked silver through young bodies to let light

drink up Simon of Trent William of Norwich

Little Saint Hugh any skipping Christ

your child! walking alone could be the

next cup of wine taken not in communion but

*libel*

his body his body his blood his body

38

# I select my own

holiness father

I can unpick it

take this salt lick this pine cone holy

this ribbed blue carpet street corner in Easton

this climbing frame wholly unsafe

anxious hinge of the seesaw

Annie Eisenthal's shins wreathed and stuttering up

to dangle like a glow worm

this stage this blank document

all of it Ginsberg'd

holy holy holy holy holy holy holy holy

the last time I typed 'holy' I missed the keys

autocorrect changed *hp; y* to *holy* before my eyes

it's that easy

## simply

apply pressure here you can break his arm
box haircut and moustaches he is belly down
on an older boy python measures goat
wreath of limbs for a mouth this is the last
judo class I will come to behind red doors
an old church flanked by walls that seemed wet
every Thursday was it size or aggression
in warm-ups he called me fat once or power
his pupils umpiring the dojo
from his sprawl *break his arm* he said it
and broke that boys arm in front of us sitting
cross-legged in a line then made us run drills

## substances deadly to goldfish

soap beer chlorine vinegar salt / a complete change of water it's hard for Goldfish to stay alive / there hasn't been enough research into the complexity of their intellectual system / to know the effect of alcohol in non-deadly doses / the effect of alcohol on humans is impaired motor functions / impedance of the adrenal gland / leading to lowered inhibitions / increased confidence and risk taking / and if alcohol use is sustained / the shutting down of the hypothalamus / goldfish is renowned for having weak short-term memory / which is true but they can learn through repetition / goldfish doesn't feel fear / goldfish tastes / fear is a taste they know in their delicate skeleton to hide from / goldfish tastes pebbles and kernels of hard mud to know what water knows / which is mostly everything / goldfish is orange because they are proud of their living body and its ability to fold on itself / seconds from every escape moving into their future too quick / human hands are complex networks of bone and tendon easily damaged which is inconvenient / but for goldfish to touch / they have to get in there with the belly / the face / all the places you typically want to protect

## I am watching

your peyot cut in the street
Hersz Laskowski in museums this photo:
four uniforms four holstered Lugers
scissors' uncareful closing your face
a brick that burns itself slow as a brick into the lens
let me be clear
                        I have not suffered this
only boy's insults cutting
without uniforms or sanctioned fingers
they met me as equals and we wrestled
with promises quick blunt exchanges and now
one threatens my hair with his scissors
so my brother rises with skinhead cut and promises

all of my lucky escapes Hersz Laskowski
to rise up in your photograph a promise
to the four; you reaching into their grins to the wrist
holding each line of teeth as Samson held the lion's and opening

## onto this scene

my grandfather spelling his name
watching the engraver; long blonde man with neat hair
pale fingers taking down details my grandfather is spelling
his name   *k, a, m, neine, m. Ya, doppelt m*
*e, r,* the engraver is playing it in his mouth
like a fish bone his spine straightening my grandfather
is watching the engraver knows in his skin
something prickling the engraver asking for the pen
to see what a Jew owns after the war
roll it in his fingers a Jewish name will be
spelled by what his machine takes away

goldfish has

a simple mouth          so their

speech in the traditional                    sense

    is     limited

the elliptical

opening and closing allows

only          plosives and bi-labials

   their     tongue too old          to work

a sibilant or fricative

growing          as they did

from simple forms:

   a     satsuma          lava

sunset     their first word is *Mum*

   or *Mom*     then *Da*

*buh* may be                    observed

for fraternal

relations          but

without     the ability to create

sibilance          they

cannot pronounce


*sister*

## my mum wanted girls

she always said
we were four boys
two in each hand I couldn't tell my brother I loved him
but I could dry slap whoever
catch an earful and a sharp fist to the chest
when I couldn't tell my three brothers
I loved them but I could put a boy
in a headlock for being overzealous whispering in his ear
how I adored them all before slipping away just to tell
one day my brother came home
and someone had hurt him in the eye and mouth
it took a year for me to show my love
a year to find that boy and announce myself and
show my love then five bigger boys showing me
their love showing me the ground where I could lie down

**the river is where**

there is set          an alphabet
          in          too-dim light
                      the ancient sling;     their     surroundings
     darken           as the land
                      ages underneath     their
          scales      glowing molten
and now               the return
          to          their stones     and
                      leaves and
                      candles
     now              we are lighting
                      the candles
                      cloth stretched                    underneath
          its         small carp
flickering            inside
                                    shocked




     blue

**now I know**

my prayers are music on the edge
of collapse alive in tongue's root
like an ache Hebrew fits messy
into song's holes audible only
in past-tense beginning in lungs
melody moves independent
through throat and mouth buried
low under diaphragms hammock
I could not pick it out of a guitar

this song with no source lives
in my body like a healthy organ
as pancreas arteries veins
capillaries and the moving parts
of my eyes which operate silent
too perfectly slotted to register
on the electric charts of synapse
with candles lit we reach inside for
words we could never picture
with only hope to shape sense
dumbblind in an hysteric wash
reach into the earth's hum with
hope and history and hope
and hope a prayer appears

# Notes

**let us say**
SA is an abbreviation of Sturmabteilung (German: "Assault Division"), also known as Storm Troopers or Brownshirts: a paramilitary branch of the Nazi party, whose methods of violent intimidation played a key role in Adolf Hitler's rise to power.

**for my grandfather the demob centre**
Kerrison is the false name on my grandparents' wartime identification papers. This adopted name was chosen to obscure their Jewishness in the hope that they could remain safe in the event of a Nazi invasion.

**look**
Quote taken from Michael Ignatieff's introduction to *Moments of Reprieve* by Primo Levi

**emerging in Theresienstadt**
Theresienstadt was a hybrid concentration camp and ghetto outside Prague. Situated in an old army barracks, conditions were marginally better than in other camps. Secret schools were set up to continue children's educations and retain a fragment of normalcy. Music recitals and theatre were also secretly organised. When the clandestine operations came to light the Nazis legalised them to some extent, using the camp as a propaganda tool for the rest of the world. From Theresienstadt, or Terezín (the name of the town), more than 88,000 Jews were transited to extermination camps, and 33,000 were murdered on the campus.

*it is not propaganda's task*
Quote attributed to Joseph Goebbels, the Nazi minister of propaganda.

**but for the louse, the baker, did you know**
Each of these sonnets is based on Nazi propaganda posters displayed in the exhibition 'Blood: Uniting and Dividing' at Krakow's Galicia Museum.

**thousands**
The painter is Frederika 'Friedl' Dicker-Brandeis, an Austrian artist and educator murdered by the Nazis in the Auschwitz-Birkenau extermination camp. She ran secret drawing and painting workshops at Theresienstadt camp, amassing more than 4000 drawings from the children imprisoned there. Some of these drawings are exhibited at the Pinkas Synagogue in Prague.

**I am watching**
Hersz Laskowski was a young Polish Jew publicly murdered by Nazi soldiers in 1942, alongside his father, Rabbi Eliasz Laskowski. He is buried in the Jewish Cemetery of Warta.

## Acknowledgments

Many thanks to Arts Council England for the grant.

Endless thanks to Katie for the support, feedback and patience. I couldn't have done it without you.

Huge gratitude to Out-Spoken Press, especially to Anthony Anaxagorou for trusting in the vaguest idea. I needed an excuse to do this and you provided it. Massive thanks to Wayne Holloway-Smith for being a direct and excellent editor, to my collaborators, Antosh Wojcik, Bel Ehresmann, Emma Houston, Si Rawlinson and Saskia Horton; we finished this book together, to Rachel Davies and Pat Haddad for the Berlin stay and the recommendations, to Claudia Rubenstein and the Jewish Book Festival for the opportunity to test the material, to Christine and Keith for making space for us during Lockdown when this book was being finished, and to the following people for encouragement, support, background noise, distraction and for generally being inspiring and/or brilliant: Rachel Nelken, Chin Keeler, Emma Tornero, Rowan Sawday, Jack Miguel, Toby King, Raymond Antrobus, Deanna Rodger, Simon Mole, Mister Gee, Joelle Taylor, Layla Wolfson, Cathy Weatherald, Tom MacAndrew, Liza Pema and everyone at number 3.

The deepest thanks to Mum, Dad, Sam, Ben, Simon, and the Kammerling and Plaschkes clans. We're all here. This book is for you as well.

And to Remi, the next chapter's yours.

## Other titles by Out-Spoken Press

*54 Questions for the Man Who Sold a Shotgun to My Father*
JOE CARRICK-VARTY

*Lasagne* • WAYNE HOLLOWAY-SMITH

*Mutton Rolls* • ARJI MANUELPILLAI

*Contains Mild Peril* • FRAN LOCK

*Epiphaneia* • RICHARD GEORGES

*Stage Invasion: Poetry & the Spoken Word Renaissance*
PETE BEARDER

*Nascent* • VOL 1: AN ANTHOLOGY

*Ways of Coping* • OLLIE O'NEILL

*The Neighbourhood* • HANNAH LOWE

*The Games* • HARRY JOSEPHINE GILES

*Songs My Enemy Taught Me* • JOELLE TAYLOR

*To Sweeten Bitter* • RAYMOND ANTROBUS

*Dogtooth* • FRAN LOCK

*How You Might Know Me* • SABRINA MAHFOUZ

*Heterogeneous, New & Selected Poems*
ANTHONY ANAXAGOROU

*Titanic* • BRIDGET MINAMORE

Email: press@outspokenldn.com